IMAGES
of America

ROUTE 66
IN NEW MEXICO

This classic arch topped with a Route 66 shield stood at the Arizona–New Mexico State Line. The westbound side offered best wishes to drivers and asked them to come again to New Mexico. It was constructed in the 1930s and demolished about the time Route 66 was widened in 1959. (Courtesy of the National Archives.)

ON THE COVER: Route 66 actually crosses itself at Fourth Street and Central Avenue in Albuquerque, the intersection of the pre-1937 alignment through Santa Fe and the post-1937 route via Central Avenue. This view is to the west from the Santa Fe Railroad overpass. The menu for the Liberty Café at right said "We will not knowingly serve minors or Indians." (Courtesy of Nancy Tucker.)

IMAGES
of America

ROUTE 66 IN NEW MEXICO

Joe Sonderman

ARCADIA
PUBLISHING

Published by Arcadia Publishing
Charleston SC, Chicago IL, Portsmouth NH, San Francisco CA

Printed in the United States of America

Library of Congress Control Number: 2009935208

For all general information contact Arcadia Publishing at:
Telephone 843-853-2070
Fax 843-853-0044
E-mail sales@arcadiapublishing.com
For customer service and orders:
Toll-Free 1-888-313-2665

Visit us on the Internet at www.arcadiapublishing.com

"We are all travelers. From birth 'til death
we travel between the eternities."
In memory of Lillian Redman

CONTENTS

ACKNOWLEDGMENTS

Thanks to Glenn Fye at the Albuquerque Museum, the members of the Route 66 E-group, and especially to Nancy Tucker. Mike Truax and Jim Coad also helped out with images. No book on Route 66 would be possible without the work of Michael Wallis, Jerry McClanahan, David Wickline, Russell Olsen, Tom Snyder, Quinta Scott, Thomas Arthur Repp, and Jim Ross. Unless otherwise credited, all images are from the author's collection.

INTRODUCTION

A traveler on Route 66 across the "Land of Enchantment" witnesses an amazing variety of culture, history, and scenery. Part of the route follows the oldest road in America, the Camino Real de Tierra Adentro, or "Royal Road to the Interior Lands." That route between Mexico City and Santa Fe has been in use since 1598. Early travelers took the path of least resistance around natural barriers hindering east-west travel, and the railroads followed.

The Fred Harvey Company opened the Southwest to mass tourism. First providing Santa Fe rail travelers with quality hotels and dining, the company began offering "Indian Detours" in 1925. Railroad travelers could take car or bus tours to visit Native American sites. The tours provided some of the impetus for improving the roads.

East-west travel was accorded little importance when a state highway system was designated in 1914. There was no east-west state route between Santa Rosa and Moriarty.

Meanwhile, private promoters were laying out highways with fancy names. Most made money from contributions by business owners to route the highway past their doors, often taking motorists miles out of their way. By 1924, there were over 250 such trails in the United States promoted by at least 100 different groups, each using their own symbols and colored markings painted on poles or any handy surface. Between Tucumcari and Santa Rosa, the Panhandle-Pacific Highway, the Atlantic-Pacific Highway, the Texas–New Mexico Highway, and the Ozark Trails Highway all shared sections of the road that would become Route 66.

In 1925, the federal government took action. The federal highway system assigned even numbers to east-west routes, with the most important routes ending in 0. North-south highways got odd numbers, the most important ending in 5. The route between Chicago and Los Angeles was designated as U.S. 60. But Gov. William J. Fields of Kentucky demanded that the more important-sounding 60 pass through his state, so 66 was assigned to the Chicago-to-Los Angeles route.

The newly formed Route 66 Association went to work promoting the road with a footrace over Route 66 from Los Angeles to Chicago and then on to New York. Promoter C. C. "Cash and Carry" Pyle charged communities to host this traveling circus. The 199 runners and an army of reporters left Los Angeles on March 4, 1928, entering New Mexico on March 28. The city of Albuquerque banned the racers, because Mayor Clyde Tingley believed Pyle and his people were crooks. The runners were forced to detour 17 miles up Tijeras Canyon before a downhill run into Moriarty. Just 93 runners were left by the time the dusty caravan made it to Glenrio. Just 55 remained when a part-Cherokee from the Route 66 town of Foyil, Oklahoma, named Andy Payne crossed the finish line on May 26. He won $25,000 and Pyle lost a pile of money, but Route 66 was front-page news. Originally, 66 turned north near today's exit 267 on Interstate 40, passing through Dilia before joining the current U.S. 84 to Romeroville. It then joined U.S. 85 to Santa Fe and along the old Camino Real to enter Albuquerque on Fourth Street, heading south to Los Lunas before finally turning west. It was a meandering route of 506 miles, of which only 28 miles were paved in 1926. The long loop avoided the sandy hills and steep grades west of the Rio Grande as well as the tire-shredding lava fields near Grants.

Completion of a Rio Grande bridge at Old Town Albuquerque in 1931 and the Rio Puerco Bridge in 1933 finally allowed travelers to head straight west and bypass Los Lunas. But that route did not become 66 until a ticked-off politician came along.

Arthur T. Hannett lost his bid for reelection as governor in 1925. Partly in revenge, he ordered construction of a highway between Santa Rosa and Albuquerque. Crews battled vandalism and terrible weather, working double shifts to finish the job in the 31 days before new governor Richard C. Dillon took office. Dillon immediately ordered the work halted, but the road had opened just hours before the order arrived.

Route 66 shifted to "Hannett's Joke" in 1937, cutting the mileage across New Mexico by 107 miles and entering Albuquerque on Central Avenue. In 1935, there were 16 tourist camps along Fourth Street and just three on Central Avenue. By 1955, there were 98 motels along Central Avenue.

The post–World War II era was the golden age of Route 66. Veterans took their families to see the wonders of the west or to seek new opportunity in California. Bobby Troup's song "Route 66" was released in 1946. It was a hit for Nat King Cole and has since been recorded by dozens of artists. From 1960 to 1964, the television series *Route 66* beamed images of the roadside into America's living rooms.

The popularity of Route 66 contributed to its demise. As speeds and traffic loads increased, the number of accidents grew. Between 1953 and 1958, one in every five highway fatalities statewide was on Route 66.

During World War II, Gen. Dwight David Eisenhower witnessed the importance of good roads to the military. President Eisenhower also saw road construction as a way to stimulate the economy. Congress passed his Federal Highway Aid Act in 1956, creating the Interstate Highway System.

Because the interstates used a different numbering system, there would be no Interstate 66. The first section of Interstate 40 in New Mexico was finished by 1960 between Santa Rosa and Clines Corners. But it would be some time before the cities were bypassed. State lawmakers passed a measure requiring community approval of a bypass. After the federal government threatened to cut off funds, the measure was repealed in 1966.

In the late 1960s, there were so many crashes on Route 66 between Glenrio and Tucumcari that it became known as "Slaughter Lane." Interstate 40 construction was delayed there due to a dispute over the route around San Jon. The interstate through Albuquerque was finished in 1970. Bypasses were completed at Santa Rosa in 1972, Moriarty in 1973, Grants in 1974, and Gallup in 1980. The section around Tucumcari and San Jon opened in 1981.

But the old road refused to die. Travelers continue to seek out the tourist traps, vintage motels, and gas stations. New Mexico should be experienced at a slower pace, where the road follows the contour of the land and trains race alongside. For those of us who think getting there is half the fun, the Land of Enchantment begins at the Interstate 40 off-ramp.

One

GLENRIO TO SANTA ROSA

Glenrio straddles the state line, where the Texas Longhorn advertised "Last Stop in Texas" on one side of its sign and "First Stop in Texas" on the other. The motel and post office were in New Mexico. Glenrio became a ghost town when Interstate 40 opened in 1973. Only friendly stray dogs greet the occasional visitor to the ruins today.

Homer and Margaret Ehresman opened the State Line Bar at Glenrio about 1934. It was on the New Mexico side of the line because Deaf Smith County, Texas, was a dry county. Margaret ran the post office. The Ehresmans left in 1946 amid rumors of an impending bypass, but they returned in 1950 to construct the Texas Longhorn.

Endee was named after the nearby ND Ranch and was reportedly a rowdy place when the ranch hands were in town. The population peaked at 187 in 1950, when the Endee Grocery and garage was thriving. Only ruins of the garage and a motor court remain today, including an old privy with "Modern Restrooms" painted on the side.

Old 66 between Glenrio and San Jon is a lonely road now covered in gravel. San Jon (pronounced "San Hone") had a population of 250 in 1946 and offered plenty of services for Route 66 travelers. The town was bypassed in 1980. Just one motel, the San Jon, was still in operation in 2010. Old Route 66 Truck and Auto Parts closed in 2004.

Tucumcari takes its name from the nearby mountain and is Comanche for "lookout." But locals concocted a legend that the braves Tonopah and Tocom fought to succeed Chief Wautonomah and marry his daughter Kari. Kari loved Tocom. When Tocom was slain in the duel, Kari stabbed Tonopah and plunged the knife into her own heart. Her father is said to have cried "Tocom-Kari" in anguish as he took his own life.

Hundreds of red billboards reading "TUCUMCARI TONITE!" lined Route 66 promoting the town with 2,000 motel rooms. Route 66 through Tucumcari was carrying up to 8,000 vehicles per day before Interstate 40 opened. It was known as Gaynell Boulevard, was renamed Tucumcari Boulevard in 1970, and became Route 66 Boulevard in 2004.

Cactus Motor Lodge
Tucumcari, New Mexico

A Western Welcome Awaits You

One-Half Mile East on U. S. Highway 66

AT THE FOOT OF THE FAMOUS INDIAN LEGENDARY TUCUMCARI MOUNTAIN

Pat and Edna Perry opened the Cactus Motor Lodge in 1941. The stucco buildings were covered with stone after Norma and Irene Wegner took over in 1952. The motel closed in the 1990s, and the courtyard was converted into an RV park. Funding from the National Park Service Route 66 Corridor Preservation Program helped restore the sign in 2008.

U.S. HIGHWAY 66... East Entrance Of ... TUCUMCARI, NEW MEXICO

The Palomino Motel opened in 1953 and was owned by James and Gladys Hyde when this view was made. They advertised "Why pay more? Please inspect our rooms. You will stay." The 30-unit Palomino is still in business today at 1215 East Highway 66. The smaller original sign is on display at Neonopolis in Las Vegas.

Del Akin and his wife, Wilma, opened Del's Restaurant in the 1940s. In 1956, it was moved west to expand and take better advantage of the Route 66 traffic. Del ran the restaurant for decades before sisters Yvonne Braziel and Yvette Peacock took over in 1995. This view was taken before the big Hereford cow was installed atop the sign.

Many tourist-related business in Tucumcari, such as the Tocom-Kari Motel, printed the romantic legend of the mountain on their postcards and brochures. Owned by Arnold and Helen Capsey and a member of United Motor Courts, the Tocom-Kari at 1110 East Highway 66 grew to include 20 units. The site is now a parking lot.

The 25-unit Apache Motel opened in 1964. The sign and exterior featured images of Kokopelli, the Hopi symbol of fertility, music, and mischief. Tepees were painted in the stairwells. The motel closed in 2005, but it has been renovated and is back in business. Unfortunately, the new owner chose to paint the background of the sign white.

The Circle S Ranch, south of Tucumcari, was one of the famous early ranch brands of New Mexico. The Circle S Motel was originally known as the Circle S Ranch Motel. John and Callie Sefcik built it, and it was later owned by Ken and Billie Dunlap. It still stands at 1010 East Highway 66 and is now the Relax Inn.

Lois and Ed Hall owned Hall's Restaurant, which stood next to the Circle S Motel at 1006 East Highway 66. Their motto was "Come as you are." The Halls advertised that hickory smoked chicken, charcoaled steak, Mexican food, Italian spaghetti, and hickory barbecue were their specialties. The Golden Dragon Chinese restaurant opened here in 1966.

Tee Pee Curios was originally a service station, grocery, and curio store owned by Leland Haynes. It opened in 1944 at 924 Highway 66. The tepee and the neon sign were added in 1960, when it became Jene Klaverweiden's Trading Post. Mike and Betty Callens have been running the store since 1985, and the sign has been restored.

W. A. Huggins began constructing the Blue Swallow Motel in 1939. Prominent rancher Ted Jones, shown here, bought it in 1942. Floyd Redman, operator of the Bonanza Motel, took over after Jones and his wife died in a plane crash. Floyd gave it to his wife, Lillian, as an engagement present in 1958, and Lillian added a larger sign in 1960.

Lillian Redman came west in a covered wagon in 1915 and worked as a Harvey Girl. Floyd Redman died in 1973, and Lillian saw the Blue Swallow Motel become a Route 66 icon. Hilda and Dale Baake took over and restored it in 1998. Lillian died in 1999. Bill Kinder and Terry Johnson now welcome travelers beneath the glow of the pink and blue neon.

Del and Wilma Akin operated the Ron-Dy-Voo Café. Del would serve as mayor of Tucumcari and go on to operate Del's Restaurant for several decades. This postcard said that about 300,000 "very welcome guests from all parts of the world" passed through the doors each year. The building at 310 East Highway 66 became the Living Word Church.

The 23-room Motel Safari at 722 East Highway 66 opened in 1960. The sign was originally topped with a Best Western logo, replaced with a camel in 1962. The Safari was later owned by Joe and Bernice Dille, Mr. and Mrs. George Strauss, and Mr. and Mrs. Ronald Frey. Richard Talley completely renovated the Safari in 2008.

La Cita restaurant opened in 1940 on the north side of Highway 66 at First Street. A new building with a sombrero-shaped entrance opened on the other side of the highway at 812 First Street in 1961. The restaurant closed in 2004 but reopened under new ownership in 2006. The eye-catching rotating neon sign featuring a sombrero is still there.

The Desert Air Motel with its classic Googie-style neon sign was built on the site of the Star Motel, which opened about 1935. It is now known as the Americana Motel at 406 East Highway 66. The sign has been changed, and the cactus on top has been replaced with AAA logo, but it is still a favorite of photographers.

Harry Harrison's café and curio stop was across from the Rock Island and Southern Pacific Railroad station. Harry met the trains wearing western garb and toting pearl-handled six-guns, escorting travelers to his café. He was immortalized in the song "Two Gun Harry from Tucumcari," a big hit for Dorothy Shay in 1948.

Bettie Ditto came to Tucumcari in 1955 to develop Lin's Motor Court, which she had inherited from her father. In 1959, she greatly expanded the court into the Congress Inn. It quickly grew into the sprawling 92-unit Best Western Pow Wow. Bettie became a civic leader known as "Mrs. Tucumcari" and died on January 5, 2008, at age 91.

Marvin and Alice Whittington built and owned several properties in Tucumcari, including the Sahara Sands Motel, Pony Soldier Motel, and La Cita restaurant. They opened the Golden W Motel in 1953 and sold it in 1957. It became the Golden Western Motel, later the Scottish Inn and the Budget Inn, at 824 West Highway 66.

They promised "Good Food Always—Always Good Food" at the Ranch House Café, which opened in 1952. It was operated by Pearl and Dugan Barnett and was one of the first to offer drive-up-style curb service. The abandoned building and its weathered sign were still standing as of 2010.

The Buckaroo Motel at 1315 West Highway 66 was built in 1952 and acquired by Ruby and Stanley Jennings in 1963. After Stanley died in 1975, Ruby ran the motel by herself until 1993. She ended up repossessing the motel several years later and ran it until 2004 before selling the Buckaroo to Shawna and Dave Meguire.

Authentic redwood was used when the L-shaped Redwood Lodge at 1502 West Highway 66 was constructed in 1954. It is believed that the expensive redwood was used to protect the structure against termites. Roger Jensen bought the Redwood in 1994 and restored the lodge, still in business next to the Tucumcari Convention Center.

The 21-unit Traveler's Paradise Motor Lodge opened about 1950 a mile west of town and was soon known simply as the Paradise Motel. Owners included Mr. and Mrs. J. E. Goodloe, John L. Lillie, and John J. Jackson. The fantastic sign featuring a diving bathing beauty has been restored to its original appearance.

Route 66 lies beneath Interstate 40 as it slopes toward the Pecos River. Nine miles east of Santa Rosa, the Frontier Museum and café, operated by William S. and C. F. Wilson, was a good old-fashioned tourist trap. Touting authentic relics of the Old West, the attraction opened in 1952. Only ruins remain today.

Lake View Courts
One-Half Mile East of — SANTA ROSA, NEW MEXICO
On U. S. Highways 66 — 54 — 84

LAKE VIEW MODERN COURTS

The Lake View Courts opened in 1941, but fell on hard times in the 1960s. Canuto Sanchez Jr. bought the property and planned to tear it down to build a Ramada Inn. But he decided to keep the motel when the news came that the interstate was about to bypass Santa Rosa. Later called the Plains Motel, it closed in 1973.

The 50-unit Surf Motel, which was a half-mile west of the Route 66 junction with U.S. 54, was billed as the finest in Santa Rosa and was a Best Western Motel. H. D. McAda and F. G. Allen owned it when these ladies, a poodle, and a pin-up photographer gathered around the heated swimming pool. The location became a Motel 6.

Lettie's Restaurant, which overlooked Santa Rosa, invited travelers to enjoy the beautiful panoramic view of the valley while dining. It was operated by Albert and Ida Jo Campos, who later ran the Adobe Inn Restaurant. This building still looks much the same, and it is now the Route 66 Restaurant at 1819 Historic Route 66.

The Sun 'n Sand Motel was owned by John Coury when this photograph was taken. The restored sign features the sacred sun symbol of the Zia Pueblo Indians. It consists of four points radiating from a circle symbolizing life. The sacred number four represented the four directions, the four seasons, parts of the day, and stages of life.

Leo and Violet McCowan had lived in Saudia Arabia, keeping their marriage a secret so Violet would be allowed to work for the government railroad. They bought the Sahara Lounge from L. G. Smith in 1957. The McCowans would run the Sahara for over 20 years. The building was still standing but boarded up in 2010.

In 1956, Jose Campos Sr. opened La Fiesta Café as a drive-in. It was enclosed in 1962–1963, and Jose passed it to his son Joseph in 1985. It is now Joseph's Bar and Grill. Joseph and Christina Campos brought back the iconic "Fat Man" logo from the Club Café, and he now smiles above Joseph's at 865 Historic Route 66.

The Western, advertised as "Santa Rosa's luxury motel," opened in 1952 at 860 Will Rogers Drive/ Highway 66. The 48-unit complex became the Milner Western Motel in 1971 and was described by AAA as having "unusually well maintained very tastefully appointed rooms." It had been closed for some time and partly demolished in 2010.

Jose and Carmen Campos opened La Loma Lodge in 1949. Later La Loma Motel, it advertised "Beautiful Franciscan Furniture, Inter Connecting rooms for family accommodations and Free Swimming Privileges." The Campos family still operates the motel today at 761 Historic Route 66, a section also known as Parker Avenue.

The 32-unit Tower Courts, later the Tower Motel, opened across from the Club Café in 1950. It was operated for many years by Ira "Smitty" Smith, who opened the Pecos Theatre in 1936. He advertised "all rooms beautifully arranged thruout with the latest Western design furnishings." The Tower Motel is still in business today.

Newton Epps founded the Club Café in 1935, naming it after the trefoil playing card suit. Phillip Craig and Ron Shaw took over in 1939 and introduced the logo that made the café famous. The smiling Fat Man, reportedly a caricature of Craig, was emblazoned on billboards along Route 66. Jim Hall designed and painted the billboards.

JACK'S CAFE "Known From Coast to Coast"
Serving The Finest Foods
Right in Town — On U. S. Highways 66-54-84
SANTA ROSA, NEW MEXICO

Craig and Shaw expanded the café and added a curio store in 1950. Ron Chavez, who had started out as a dishwasher, took over in May 1973 and closed it down in 1992. Joseph and Christina Campos hoped to restore the building, but it was too far gone and was demolished in 2005. But the Fat Man lives on at Joseph's, just a half block away.

In his famous *A Guide Book to Highway 66*, published in 1946, Jack Rittenhouse recommended Jack's Café. The first Jack's location was in Tucumcari, and the Santa Rosa location opened about 1940. Jack's was known for sizzling steaks. The building still stands on Fourth Street across from the courthouse.

During the heyday of Route 66, there were over 60 gas stations, 20 motels, and 15 restaurants in Santa Rosa. This view looks east into town from the Pecos River Bridge. In the film *The Grapes of Wrath*, Tom Joad (Henry Fonda) watched a train steam into the sunset on the adjacent railroad bridge.

From 1926 until 1937, Route 66 ran past the Blue Hole, an oasis for travelers and now a popular destination for scuba divers. This natural artesian well is surrounded by sandstone. The Blue Hole is 81 feet deep, with water of amazing clarity and a constant temperature of 61 degrees. A spring supplies 3,000 gallons of water per minute.

The Comet II Drive-In began as a tiny food and drink stand that opened in 1950. It was expanded and became Mucho Burger in 1955. Johnny Martinez purchased the restaurant in 1961, and it became the Comet Drive-In. Johnny and Alice Martinez still run the restaurant, renamed Comet II after an expansion, at 217 Parker Avenue.

In 1947, the 22-unit Rancho Motor Lodge opened just west of the Pecos River Bridge. H. D. "Mac" McAda and partner J. M. Fields constructed it. McAda would also own the Santa Rosa Courts and went on to build the Ramada Inn in 1961. The Rancho was later owned by W. M. Medley and has been demolished.

Two

ROUTE 66 THROUGH SANTA FE 1926–1937

A traveler snapped this image of the Arrowhead Camp at Glorieta on July 4, 1929. It consisted mostly of log structures and included a gas station, store, and cabins that cost 50¢ per night in the 1930s. After the Santa Fe alignment of Route 66 was eliminated, it became the Arrowhead Lodge. Only ruins remain today.

Alexander Valle was a Frenchman who spoke pidgin or "pigeon" English. His Pigeon Ranch was a stage stop on the Santa Fe Trail and served as a field hospital during the Civil War battle of Glorieta Pass on May 28, 1862. Thomas L. Greer made it a tourist attraction in 1924 and it closed in the 1940s. The main building and the well remain.

Conquistador Don Pedro de Peralta laid out La Villa de La Santa Fe de San Francisco (Royal City of the Holy Faith of St. Francis) in 1609. Originally, 66 used the Old Santa Fe Trail, San Francisco, Don Gaspar, and De Vargas Streets. In 1931, the route shifted to bypass the plaza, eventually following Water and Galisteo Streets to Cerillos Road. (Courtesy of Mike Truax.)

The San Miguel Mission is the oldest continuously occupied church in the United States. It was constructed between 1610 and 1628 by Tlaxcala Indians brought to New Mexico as servants to the Spanish. The structure incorporated parts of a pueblo dating back to about 1100. It was burned during the 1680 Pueblo Revolt and rebuilt by the Spanish in 1710.

This building is said to be the oldest house in the United States. The adobe structure dates back to around 1646, but is said to have been built on the remnants of an 800-year-old pueblo. The original second floor was removed in 1902 and then replaced in 1929. It was restored in 2003 as part of the Hampton Inn "Save a Landmark" program.

An inn or *fonda* has occupied the southeast corner of the plaza since 1610. The current La Fonda was built in 1922. The Atchison, Topeka, and Santa Fe Railroad leased it to the Fred Harvey Company in 1926, and it became one of the famous Harvey Houses. Mike Ballen bought it in 1968, and the family still runs La Fonda. (Courtesy of Mike Truax.)

Built in 1610, the Palace of the Governors, on the north side of the plaza, is the oldest occupied public building in the United States. It was besieged by Pueblo Indians for five days during the 1680 revolt. The Spanish governors ruled from here from 1692 to 1822, the Mexican regime from 1822 to 1846, and the U.S. territorial governors from 1846 to 1907.

The adobe-styled El Rey Auto Court (now El Rey Inn) opened in 1936 with 12 rooms. El Rey expanded in the 1950s, and the carports between the rooms were enclosed. Terrell White acquired the court in 1973 and expanded to take in the adjacent Alamo Lodge property in 1994.

The route over La Bajada Mesa (Spanish for "the descent") was part of the Camino Real. The road was rebuilt in 1908 by Cochiti Indians and convict labor. It drops 800 feet in 1.6 miles with 23 hairpin switchbacks. A sign at the top warned "this road is not foolproof but safe for a sane driver." La Bajada was bypassed in 1932. (Courtesy of Nancy Tucker.)

The Seligman family established the Santo Domingo Trading Post in 1881, and an adobe-style addition was constructed in 1922. Fred and Alicia Thompson took over in 1949. Pres. John F. Kennedy visited on December 7, 1962. A fire on February 12, 2001, nearly destroyed the trading post, but plans for rehabilitation are moving forward.

South of Santo Domingo, Route 66 passed through this 18-foot-wide, 75-foot-long cut through Gravel Hill on El Camino Real. The "Big Cut" was considered an engineering marvel when it was dug out in 1909. Route 66 was rerouted in 1931, but the cut is still visible from Interstate 25, behind San Felipe's Casino Hollywood.

Route 66 originally entered Albuquerque on Fourth Street, where there were 19 tourist courts prior to the 1937 realignment of Route 66 over Central Avenue. Only El Camino Motor Hotel is still operating today. The Albuquerque Auto Court was located at 2050 North Fourth Street and operated by C. W. Gruhn. (Courtesy of Nancy Tucker.)

In 1929, Oklahoma oilman R. H. Robinson spent over $100,000 to construct the King's Rest Tourist Park, later King's Rest Courts, at 1816 North Fourth Street. It had 21 rooms and 17 cottages and offered amenities that were rare at the time, such as complete kitchens. It became the Interstate Inn, which was shut down by the city and demolished in 2005.

The Daughters of the American Revolution placed *Madonna of the Trail* statues in each of the 12 states along the National Old Trails Road. Santa Fe turned down the offer, and the statue was dedicated in McClellan Park on September 27, 1928. When the new U.S. courthouse was constructed, the statue was moved to the northwest corner of the site. (Courtesy of Mike Truax.)

Charles Wright's first trading post opened on Central Avenue in 1907. This pueblo-styled building at Fourth Street and Gold Avenue was built in 1920. Wright died in 1938, and his wife sold the business to Sam and Marguerite Chernoff in 1958. Wright's Indian Art is still in business, but this structure was torn down in 1959 for the New Mexico Bank and Trust Building, also known as the Gold Building. (Courtesy of Albuquerque Museum.)

Virgil Katsanis, who later changed his name to Bob Katson, opened the Court Café on November 4, 1925. This jet-black carrera glass facade was added in January 1935. Elmer and Rosa Lea Elliott operated it from 1945 to 1958. It changed names several times before becoming the Fourth Street Café in 1991 and is now Ralli's Fourth Street Bar and Grill.

From 1926 to 1937, Route 66 continued on Fourth Street to Bridge Street, to the Barelas Bridge over the Rio Grande, and then south on Isleta Boulevard. They advertised "Courtesy is the motto" at the DeLuxe Modern Auto Camp, on two shady acres along the river at 508 Bridge Street. It was demolished in 1958, when the road was widened.

Originally, Route 66 continued south past the Isleta Pueblo to Los Lunas. The Spanish Mission of San Agustin de la Isleta was established in 1612, and the church was rebuilt in 1716. Completion of the Rio Puerco Bridge in 1933 allowed traffic to head straight west from Albuquerque, and the "Laguna Cut-off" became part of Route 66 in 1937.

Three

HANNETT'S JOKE

Clines Corners on Highway 66, New Mexico

In 1934, Roy Cline erected a tiny gas station at the intersection of New Mexico Route 6 (Hannett's Santa Fe bypass) and New Mexico Route 2. When the bypass became U.S. 66 in 1937, Roy moved the building 11 miles to the intersection of U.S. 66 and U.S. 285. He convinced Rand McNally to put Clines Corners on their maps.

CLINES CORNERS
At the Overpass Where U. S. 285 Meets U. S. 66
New Mexico's Most Popular Highway Stopping Place
CAFE, CURIO SHOP AND SERVICE STATION

Roy sold the place in 1939, but the name stayed since it was on the maps. Lynn and Helen Smith took over after World War II and expanded, adding the distinctive neon sign. Clines Corners has its own post office and homes for employees. It remains a popular stop on Interstate 40, retaining the feel of the old tourist traps.

After selling Cline's Corners, Roy Cline opened another business in 1945, the Flying C Ranch. He ran the gas station, garage, and café 77 miles east of Albuquerque until 1963, and it became Bowlin's Flying C Ranch. Claude M. Bowlin started trading with the American Indians in 1912, and the family business has since grown to 12 travel centers.

Capt. Bill Ehret was a former police officer in Endicott, New York, and a former deputy in Lincoln County, New Mexico. He opened a trading post, gas station, and café 48 miles east of Albuquerque in December 1940. His Longhorn Ranch grew into a classic Route 66 roadside attraction, billed as "Where the West Still Lives."

The Longhorn Ranch gave tourists the Old West they had seen in the movies. It included a motel, restaurants, a garage, and a curio shop. There was a stage for American Indian dances. Kids could take a ride in a Concord stagecoach and see a Texas longhorn steer named Babe. The Longhorn Ranch closed in 1977, and almost no trace remains.

Hubert Odell "Blackie" Ingram had to borrow money to make change on the first day his café opened in 1945. But his entertaining character made Blackie's a Route 66 landmark. Blackie died in 1966, and his wife, Norma, kept the business going until 1975. Blackie's Bar and Grill was later constructed on the site at 612 Route 66.

The Lariat Lodge opened in 1957, consisting of 11 modern units with steam heat, television, a good restaurant, and a Texaco service station. It was owned and operated by Paul and May Dannevik when this view was made and was later owned by Hazel and Gene Hanks. It is now the Lariat Motel and was recently restored.

In 1917, Art and Ernest Whiting began selling gasoline at their Ford dealership in St. Johns, Arizona. The Whiting Brothers chain grew to over 100 stations, a familiar sight on Route 66 from Shamrock, Texas, to Barstow, California. Only one remains in business with the original signage, located in Moriarty and operated by Sal Lucero since 1985.

Military pilot Bill Pogue married a weather girl who guided the fliers over the nearby mountains. Bill and Elaine owned the house on the property now occupied by Sal Lucero's station and sold it to construct the Sunset Motel. Elaine later became mayor of Moriarty. Her son Mike and daughter-in-law Debbie Pogue still own the motel today.

Charles M. McPherson served as a chief warrant officer in the army and met his wife, Maria, while stationed in Germany. When Charles retired in 1952, they came to Moriarty and opened the 12-unit Cactus Motel. It was later owned and operated by Carl and Lorine Cravens and is now the Cactus Mall.

Moriarty is named after the first postmaster, Michael Moriarty. The community of Buford developed when Route 66 was built just north of town in 1937 and became part of Moriarty when the city incorporated in 1953. Mike Anaya's store opened in 1949 and is still there, next to El Comedor restaurant and its "Rotosphere" or Sputnik-style sign.

Route 66 travelers used to say if you made it up Sedillo Hill it was downhill all the way to California. Comer's coffee shop and truck stop stood at the top and was owned by Marie and Werner Eisenhut during its heyday. It was in business into the late 1960s but apparently didn't survive the arrival of Interstate 40 in 1970. (Courtesy of Jim Coad.)

Route 66 originally made a dangerously sharp, blind turn at the top of a hill near Carnuel known as "Dead Man's Curve." Completed in 1952, the most expensive roadway project in the history of New Mexico blasted a four-lane divided highway through the canyon and eliminated the curve. Interstate 40 wiped out the entire hill in 1965.

Tijeras Canyon separates the Sandia and the Manzano mountain ranges. The shape of the canyon resembles a pair of scissors, or "tijeras" in Spanish. The roadway drops 2,000 feet through the rugged canyon between Sedillo and Albuquerque. Raymond and Vera Curtis ran The Oasis here from 1932 until it was wiped out by Interstate 40.

Elephant Rock served as a landmark to travelers for centuries, letting them know that the journey to Albuquerque was nearly over. When the trail grew into a highway, the rock was painted with advertisements. In the 1970s, a road crew unceremoniously bulldozed the ancient landmark into the gully where it lies today.

Four

ROUTE 66 THROUGH ALBUQUERQUE

Don Francisco Cuervo y Valdes, interim governor of New Mexico, established La Villa de San Francisco Xavier de Alburquerque in 1706. The villa was named after the viceroy of New Spain, Don Francisco Fernandez de la Enriquez, eighth Duke of Alburquerque (the extra R disappeared over the years).

CURIOS

SEE THE LARGEST COVERED WAGON IN THE WORLD
ALBUQUERQUE, NEW MEXICO

This giant concrete-and-wood wagon pulled by papier-mâché oxen stood in front of Manny Goodman's Covered Wagon Souvenirs. Displaced by Interstate 40 in 1959, he moved to Old Town Plaza. Known as the "Mayor of Old Town," Goodman greeted Elvis Presley and former Pres. Bill Clinton before closing in 1998. Goodman died in 2004.

Albuquerque's first theme park, Little Beaver Town, opened on July 15, 1961. Fred Harman Jr. of Albuquerque, who drew the *Red Ryder–Little Beaver* comic strip, was a partner in the recreated Old West town. It was bankrupt by 1964, renamed Sage City, and used for commercials and local movies before being destroyed by fire and vandalism. (Courtesy of Nancy Tucker.)

The Western Skies Motel opened on March 31, 1959. Pres. John F. Kennedy stayed here on December 7, 1962. Once the most glamorous motel in Albuquerque, the Western Skies fell into disrepair. It was abandoned and then finally torn down in 1988. The site is now the Four Hills Shopping Center. (Courtesy of Gary Francis.)

The 18-unit Canyon Motel at 13001 East Central Avenue advertised, "Where comfort is assured year round." Mr. and Mrs. Baxter E. Caviness owned the motel. But the pretty little motel became notorious for its role in the horrific 1986 murder of Linda Lee Daniels. It was demolished in 2002, and the Value Place Central Hotel is located here.

La Puerta, Spanish for "the door," was modeled after the Palace of the Governors in Santa Fe and opened in 1949. The office featured a massive hand-carved door. La Puerta was owned by Ralph and Sadie Smith. Charles and Beulah Hill bought it in 1956, and the motel at 9710 East Central Avenue was still being run by the family in 2010.

The Luna Lodge at 9119 East Central Avenue, with its lovely shaded grounds, opened in 1949 and was owned by John Jelso and his wife, Dorothy. It originally had eight rooms, expanded to 26 by 1952. A swimming pool was added in 1954. Suresh Patel acquired the Luna Lodge in 1980 and kept it in business. It is now mostly monthly rentals.

In 1946, the Piñon Lodge opened at 8501 East Central Avenue. It later became the Piñon Motel. Owners included Mr. and Mrs. E. R. Kirkpatrick, Mr. and Mrs. Roy L. Welch, and Fred Mathis. The Piñon is the New Mexico state tree, and its nuts were once a staple of the Southwestern Indian diet. It is now the Piñon Motel and Apartments.

The Bow and Arrow Lodge at 8300 East Central Avenue was originally the 25-unit Urban Motor Lodge, opened in 1941 and owned by Mr. and Mrs. L. F. Morgans. Later owners of the so-called "Luxury Motel of Distinction" included Mr. and Mrs. J. L. Crow and Nadia Crow Dillon as well as Mr. and Mrs. Clinton Turnham. It is still in business today.

David Bettin opened the 47-unit El Jardin Lodge at 8100 East Central Avenue in 1946 and advertised it as "Tomorrow's Hotel Today." He had sold it to Mildred Markey by 1952, but Bettin would buy and sell the motel four times. Late in its life, it became the Route 66 Motel before closing in 2004 and being demolished in 2005.

The Pioneer Motel at 7600 East Central Avenue was originally known as the Pioneer Luxury Court and opened in 1949. It advertised "Luxury Costs no More." Originally owned by Mr. and Mrs. Bogan Higgs, it was owned by R. L. Porrata in 1958. The Pioneer, with its pretty neon sign, is still in business today.

Oscar L. Stephens owned the Loma Verde Court at 7503 East Central Avenue from the time it opened until his death in 1962. He advertised "An air conditioned modern motor court close to shopping center and all conveniences." It later became the Loma Verde Motel and still stands today. The sign has been painted green.

John and Agnes Farr originally owned the Zuni Motor Lodge at 7218 East Central Avenue. The lodge advertised "Every Comfort and Service to the Seasoned Traveler." The Spanish Colonial–style motor lodge originally consisted of 24 units and was later expanded to 40. The Zuni no longer stands.

The pueblo-styled Tewa Lodge at 5715 East Central Avenue opened in 1946, was designed by S. V. Patrick, and was owned by H. C. Harvey. It was later owned by Mr. and Mrs. Robert Daly and by a partnership that included Sen. Edward Mechem. The Tewa Lodge is still in business and is listed on the National Register of Historic Places.

Leonard and Margaret Grossman opened Leonard's restaurant in 1949, expanding in 1952. Leonard's was a popular spot for receptions and civic functions. It became Johnny Farmer's Restaurant in 1961 and then the 400 Club. A suspicious fire destroyed the club in September 1963, and the site at 6616 East Central Avenue is now a used car lot.

East On Highway 66   ALBUQUERQUE, NEW MEXICO

NOD-A-WHILE MOTOR LODGE

The cleverly named Nod-A-While Motor Lodge at 5508 East Central Avenue opened in 1946 and was operated by E. C. Grober. Advertised as a "modern motor lodge," it became the Silver Spur Motel by 1952. The Silver Spur changed hands several times during the 1950s. It was still standing in 2010 as the Lazy M Motel.

HONEY DEW DRIVE INN

5500 East Central Ave., Albuquerque, N. M. on Highway U. S. 66

The Honey Dew Drive-Inn at 5500 East Central Avenue specialized in "Steaks- Chicken-in Basket, Hamburger-Supreme" and "Glorified Ham and Eggs." The building was later expanded and housed the Chez Hubert restaurant. It became the El Cid lounge about 1968 but no longer stands. The site is now a parking lot.

Calvin and H. B. Horn opened a truck stop at 5400 East Central Avenue in 1940 and began building the $1-million, 81-unit Tradewinds Motor Hotel in February 1958. The Horns spent months studying motels along highways seeking ways to improve on existing designs. It became the Travelodge Mid Town but was torn down in 2009.

Carl McAdams opened Mac's Iceberg frozen custard stand on May 27, 1931, at 3015 East Central Avenue. It became a service station in 1934. In 1936, the wood-frame-and-plaster berg was relocated to 5219 East Central, where it housed the Iceberg Café. The landmark was trucked to U.S. 85 at Bernalillo in 1953 and became the "Iceburg" café, demolished in the 1960s. (Courtesy of Nancy Tucker.)

The Sandias, as you will see from Cooksey Court,
East on Highway 66, Albuquerque, New Mexico

R. F. "Cooksey" Kooken operated the Cooksey Court at 5210 East Central Avenue. The 17-unit motel was later operated by Ray Nathan and James P. Cleary. Two people could stay here for $3.50 in 1947. The Cooksey Court later became the New Mexico Motel. The site is now occupied by a convenience store.

The Desert Sands Motel at 5000 East Central Avenue opened on October 11, 1954. Some guests think room 109 may be haunted. They report hearing strange noises and claim the television, water, and lights mysteriously turn on and off. The Desert Sands made a bloody appearance in the movie *No Country for Old Men* disguised as a motel in El Paso, Texas.

Crest-Hi Restaurant
GOOD FOOD — ALWAYS
4805 E. Central   Albuquerque, N. M.
On Highway 66

Across the street from
The Hiland Theater

The Crest Hi Restaurant was located at 4805 East Central Avenue, across the street from the Hiland Theatre. It opened about 1952 and was remodeled in 1956. The Crest Hi advertised "complete dining services at moderate prices" and "the best cuppa coffee on Route 66." The building was occupied by a finance company in 2010.

Frank Peloso and family opened the 875-seat Hiland Theatre at 4804 East Central Avenue in 1951. The building initially stood alone, but storefront wings were later added. Bernalillo County took over the shuttered theater in 2004. In 2009, it was leased to the National Dance Institute of New Mexico, and renovation began.

The Zia Lodge, at 4611 East Central Avenue, opened in 1938 and enticed guests with "Safe steam heat, tiled baths, electric refrigeration," and "furnishings of the highest quality." After it closed in 2002, the boarded-up Zia Lodge became crime-ridden, and it burned in December 2003. It was demolished in 2005 and replaced by apartments.

Advertised as "Facing the Beautiful Sandias," the Ambassador Lodge at 4501 East Central Avenue opened in 1947. It was owned by Mr. and Mrs. Phillip Belknap and later by Jerry and Yvette Sparlin. In 1954, Felix Hickman expanded it into the American Inn. It deteriorated into a haven for criminals before being torn down in 2006.

Travelers could eat inside a giant hat at El Sombrero, located at 4415 East Central Avenue. Opened in 1949, El Sombrero offered curb service and claimed to serve 250,000 visitors annually. Owner Sherman Anderson closed down in March 1958, and the building was demolished. A bank was constructed on the site. (Courtesy of Mike Truax.)

Zuni trader Charles Garrett Wallace and S. D. Hambaugh built the lavish De Anza Motor Lodge in 1939. It was named for the Spanish lieutenant Juan Bautista de Anza, the territorial governor who saved the Hopi pueblo from starvation. The City of Albuquerque purchased the shuttered landmark in 2003, but it has yet to be restored.

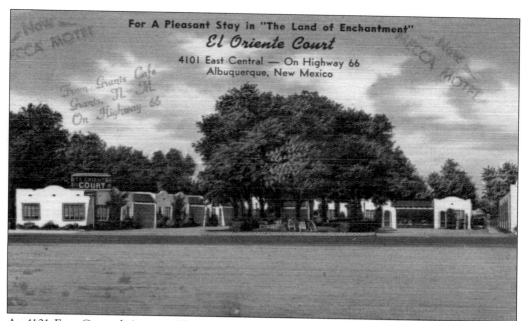

For A Pleasant Stay in "The Land of Enchantment"

El Oriente Court

4101 East Central — On Highway 66
Albuquerque, New Mexico

At 4101 East Central Avenue, El Oriente Court opened in 1935 and was owned by James R. Evans. It later became the Mecca Court and then the Minton Lodge, advertised in 1955 as "one of the newer and finer lodges in Albuquerque [with] all rooms facing shaded, restful patio for the convenience of guests." It is currently the Town Lodge.

Gwynn and Claudine Hoyt opened the Dinner Bell restaurant in 1943. The structure at 3900 East Central Avenue was greatly expanded in 1959. Charlie Preston and Rob Berg took over in 1974, opening the castle-shaped Wellington Restaurant and Lounge. A spectacular arson explosion and fire destroyed it on February 28, 1976.

The Comfort Lodge at 4020 East Central Avenue was advertised in 1952 as a "new and very attractively furnished motel, located in the uptown shopping district." It was owned by Mr. and Mrs. E. C. Ryan and by Mac and Eva McGinnis from 1952 to 1960. As of 2010, the building was occupied by Transitional Living Services.

The Aztec Court, now Aztec Motel, is the oldest continuously operated Route 66 motel in New Mexico. Guy and May Fargo opened it in 1931, six years before Central Avenue became Route 66. It was renovated by Mohamed Natha in 1991. The exterior is now a work of art, decorated with knickknacks, religious icons, coins, and shards of pottery.

Advertised as "Not the largest but the best," the Premiere Motel at 3820 East Central Avenue was constructed in 1941 with 30 rooms, later expanded to 35. In 1954, Howard and Marie Dendinger sold it to Manly and Dorothy Betts, former owners of the Conchas Motel in Tucumcari. Fire swept the vacant motel on May 23, 2009.

The Ralph Jones Motor Company Ford dealership and Texaco station was designed by Tom Danahy and opened on November 18, 1939. The building at 3222 East Central Avenue housed several businesses after the dealership moved in 1957. Dennis and Janice Bonfantine opened Kelly's Brew Pub here in 2000. (Courtesy of Albuquerque Museum.)

NOB HILL MOTEL
3712 CENTRAL, SOUTHEAST
ALBUQUERQUE, NEW MEXICO

Nob Hill was Albuquerque's first suburb, where development began in 1916. The Nob Hill Motel was originally the Modern Auto Court, built in 1936 at 3712 East Central Avenue. It closed in 2006 and was redeveloped into offices and retail stores while retaining its historic integrity. The sign was also restored.

SIDE VIEW SHOWING STORES ON S. CARLISLE

NOB HILL
BUSINESS
CENTER
3500 EAST CENTRAL
ALBUQUERQUE, N. M.

NEWEST
Most Modern and
CONVENIENT
Shopping Center

SIDE VIEW SHOWING STORES ON S. AMHERST

R. C. Waggoman opened the first suburban shopping center in Albuquerque at Carlisle Boulevard and East Central Avenue in 1947. Designed by Louis Hesseldon, the Nob Hill Business Center was criticized as "Waggoman's Folly." Today Nob Hill is the trendiest area in Albuquerque, a mix of chic shops, galleries, restaurants, and night spots.

In 1936, the federal Works Progress Administration funded construction of Fire Station No. 3 at 3205 East Central Avenue. E. H. Blumenthol, designer of the old airport and Highland High School, designed the building. It became the Monte Vista Fire Station Restaurant in 1985. (Courtesy of Nancy Tucker.)

Del Webb founded the Hiway House hotel chain in 1956. The location at 3200 East Central Avenue is the last one still operating. Webb co-owned the New York Yankees, constructed the Sun City Retirement Community in Arizona, and built the Flamingo Hotel in Las Vegas for Bugsy Siegel. Webb also owned the Mint and the Sahara casinos.

The intersection of Girard and Monte Vista Boulevards with Central Avenue is known as the Triangle. The Lobo Theatre, at right, opened on August 19, 1938. It closed in 2000 and was renovated by a church group. The vintage Little House Diner now stands in place of the Standard station. It was relocated from downtown in the 1990s and serves as a police substation.

The University of New Mexico was founded in 1889. University president William Tight (1901–1909) was fired partly for adopting the now famous Pueblo Revival architecture. John Gaw Meem designed many of the buildings in the 1930s, including Scholes Hall, the UNM Alumni Chapel, Mitchell Hall, and the Zimmerman Library.

Charley's Pig Stand opened in 1924 across from the University of New Mexico at 2106 East Central Avenue. The building shown here was constructed in 1935 and closed in 1954. Later occupied by the Lobo Laundry, the building now houses a restaurant, and the pig images are still visible on the facade.

Alma Patton opened the Dixie Barbecue at 1720 East Central Avenue in 1935. "Oklahoma" Joe Feinsilver changed the name to Oklahoma Joe's in 1941 and ran the restaurant until 1956. It evolved into Okie's, a bar popular with UNM students and known for 10¢ beer nights. A convenience store stands here today.

The Route 66 Diner opened in 1987 in the former Sam's Phillips 66 station, constructed in 1946. The diner at 1405 East Central Avenue was a huge success both with locals and Route 66 travelers. On May 23, 1995, it was destroyed by fire. Owner Tom Willis quickly rebuilt, and the diner opened again on February 5, 1996.

Looking west on Central Avenue from South Oak Street in 1943, Memorial Hospital, at left, was originally constructed to care for Santa Fe Railroad workers. The hospital closed in 1982 and then housed a psychiatric facility that closed in 2007. Developer David Oberstein converted the old hospital into the Hotel Parq Central in 2010. (Courtesy of Library of Congress.)

Albuquerque, New Mexico

This view was taken in 1961 near the same spot as the previous photograph, looking west on Central Avenue from the new Pan American Freeway (Interstate 25). The Chalet Motel at right is now the Econolodge. Behind it is the LorLodge, now the Stardust Inn. South Oak Street is now a one-way frontage road for Interstate 25.

The Vance Carothers and D. D. Fuller (originally Carothers and Maudlin) station opened in 1938 at 320 East Central Avenue. It later became a BMW dealership. Matt DiGregory and his brothers Chris, John, and Vince purchased the vacant building and opened the upscale Standard Diner here in March 2006. (Courtesy of Albuquerque Museum.)

The Alvarado Hotel opened on May 11, 1902. The famous Harvey Girls served travelers at the rambling California Mission Revival–style structure. Charles F. Whittlesey designed the hotel and depot. The hotel was named for Hernando Alvarado, Francisco de Coronado's commander of artillery. Despite the efforts of citizen groups and politicians, the Atchinson, Topeka, and Santa Fe Railroad began demolishing the landmark on February 13, 1970. The appalling loss spurred a preservation movement in Albuquerque. (Courtesy of Mike Truax.)

This view looks toward the Alvarado Hotel from the adjoining Santa Fe Depot. The 118-room hotel was the crown jewel of the Fred Harvey system and the social center of Albuquerque. A Fred Harvey Company brochure described its secluded gardens and "wide verandas overlooking beautiful sunny plazas and pools."

The Fred Harvey Company created a market for American Indian art and crafts as well as a bridge between cultures. Amazing handmade rugs, pottery, jewelry, baskets, and blankets were sold at the Indian Building, adjacent to the Alvarado Hotel. Travelers exiting the trains could see demonstrations by these craftspeople and artisans while learning about American Indian culture. (Courtesy of Library of Congress.)

The famous *Super Chief* is shown here at Santa Fe depot. The "Train of the Stars" ran between Chicago and Los Angeles from 1937 to 1974. The depot was constructed in 1902 and destroyed by fire in 1993. Today's Alvarado Transportation Center closely resembles the old structures, and the bus station was modeled after the original depot. (Courtesy of Library of Congress.)

In Albuquerque it's the

HILTON HOTEL

New Mexico's Newest and Finest

Conrad Nicholson Hilton's empire began at his parent's simple inn and general store in Socorro County, New Mexico. The Albuquerque Hilton Hotel was his fourth high rise, opening on June 9, 1931. Hilton sold the 160-room structure in 1969. It became La Posada de Albuquerque in 1984 and is now the Andaluz Hotel.

Central Avenue and Fourth Street is the heart of Albuquerque. Fourth Street was U.S. 66 from 1926 to 1937 and also carried U.S. 85. It is now a pedestrian mall between Central and Tijeras Avenues. Central Avenue was originally U.S. 470 east of Fourth Street and New Mexico 6 west of Fourth Street. U.S. 470 became U.S. 366 in 1932 and Central Avenue became U.S. 66 in 1937.

Railroad Avenue connected Old Town to New Albuquerque, which developed around the depot after the railroad arrived in 1880. It also became known as "TB Avenue," as facilities opened to serve an influx of tuberculosis (TB) patients. The name was changed to Central Avenue in 1907. A blaze of neon greeted the Route 66 traveler at night.

Looking east on Central Avenue at Fourth Street, The taller structure at right is the Rosenwald Building, home of McClellan's Five and Dime from 1927 to 1977. Woolworth's opened in 1915, and the building at left was completed in 1941. The tallest structure at left is the First National Bank Building, completed in 1922.

MAISEL'S INDIAN TRADING POST — 510 W. Central Ave. — ALBUQUERQUE, NEW MEXICO

Maurice Maisel opened his new Indian Trading Post at 510 West Central Avenue on June 23, 1939. John Gaw Meem designed the building. Maisel's employed as many as 300 craftsmen on site and became the largest American Indian jewelry store in the Southwest before closing in the 1960s. Skip Maisel reopened his grandfather's store in the 1980s.

The KiMo Theatre opened on September 19, 1927, and was built by Oreste Bachechi and designed by Carl Boller. The name is loosely translated as Tewa for "King of its Kind." The KiMo closed in 1968, and the city began restoration in 1977. The KiMo is said to be haunted by the ghost of six-year-old Bobby Darnell, who died in a boiler explosion there in 1951.

Stars such as John Wayne and Clara Bow checked into the Franciscan Hotel at Sixth Street and Central Avenue. The "pueblo expressionist" structure was dedicated on December 15, 1923. Many big band legends performed in the ballroom. The Franciscan closed on October 5, 1970, and the final section came down on June 23, 1972.

The San Felipe de Neri Church dominates the plaza in Old Town, where the Villa de Alburquerque was established in 1706. Because development shifted east to New Albuquerque with the arrival of the railroad, Old Town kept much of its historic charm. The church was built in 1793 and the Gothic steeples added in 1863.

Old Town today houses 130 shops and restaurants. La Placita opened in 1931 in a hacienda built in 1706. Don Ambrosio Armijo added a second floor in 1872, designing a staircase to be as long as the train of his daughter's wedding gown. Elmer and Rosa Lea Elliot took over in 1950, and the family still runs La Placita Dining Rooms.

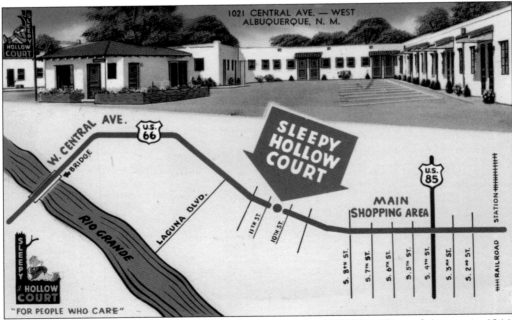

"For People Who Care," the Sleepy Hollow Court opened at 1023 West Central Avenue in 1944. It offered 27 units of "comfort and convenience to the most exacting traveler." It was owned by Mr. and Mrs. Louis T. Higgins when this view was mailed in 1951. The structure still stands but apparently is no longer a hotel.

Frank Mead and his family ran the original Dog House on Tenth Street at Central Avenue for 18 years beginning in the 1940s. The sign atop the current Dog House at 1216 West Central Avenue is from the original location and dates from about 1950. The neon dachshund happily wags his tail while downing a string of sausages.

Franz Huning helped bring the railroad to Albuquerque and platted the first subdivision, the Huning Highlands. He built this elaborate home at Fourteenth Street and Railroad Avenue (later Central Avenue) in 1883. It later housed a private school and then was demolished in 1955. The Huning Highland Apartments on the site were modeled after the castle.

This streamline moderne service station at 1717 West Central Avenue was originally operated by Glenn Hoefgen and Ralph Branson. They fought price wars with the Hedges Oil Company station across the street, selling gas for 12.9¢ per gallon in 1941. It became the World Court station in 1941 and later became Howard's Drive-In.

Calvin and Hosier B. Horn started out with one station in Albuquerque in 1938. Their business grew to include 28 stations. The Horn Oil Company and Motor Lodge at 1720 West Central Avenue opened in 1946. The motor lodge was torn down in 2006, but the rest of the complex still stands.

Some of the rooms at the Wigwam Court, at 2014 West Central Avenue, were topped with a wigwam design. By 1948, it had become the Arrowhead Lodge, and the designs changed to arrowheads. Remodeled by owners Mr. and Mrs. Palmer Peterson in 1953, it was later operated by Linton and Margaret Truman. Law offices are located here today.

Ben F. Shear constructed the streamline moderne Tower Court at 2210 West Central Avenue in 1939. A 30-foot stepped tower served as the office for the 15-room motel, one of the first "air cooled" motels in Albuquerque. The tower was removed decades ago, and the old motel is now monthly rentals.

El Don Motel at 2222 West Central Avenue opened in 1946 and originally had 15 units. Dan Eitzen sold El Don in 1958 to Rolly and Marian Pease and then constructed the Capri Motel at Twelfth Street and Central Avenue. El Don is still in business today, and the neon sign with a cowboy on the top has been restored.

In 1946, Joe Ray Calloway constructed the Texas Ann Motel at what is now 2305 West Central Avenue, reportedly naming it after a tall blonde Texan he knew with diamonds set in her front teeth. It was featured in a 1955 episode of *I Love Lucy*, which costarred Vivian Vance of Albuquerque. The motel was demolished in 1976.

The Moon Café at 2316 West Central Avenue was open around the clock and advertised that there were eight first-class motels within a couple of blocks. The café was so popular that those motel owners complained about truckers blocking Route 66. The owner moved the business in 1961, and the site is now a vacant lot.

"In the Center of the better tourist courts," the White Way was constructed in 1937 at 2321 West Central Avenue. James and Ruth Doake advertised "It's Okey Doke to Stop with the Doakes" and said it was "where tired tourists and good beds meet." It later became the Safari Lodge, and the Econo Lodge Old Town occupies the site today.

The Monterey Court at 2402 West Central Avenue opened in 1946 and was originally the Davis Court. AAA recommended the 15-unit motel operated by H. C. Whitfield, describing the rooms as "extremely well kept." It is now the Monterey Non-Smokers Motel and is still very highly recommended for Route 66 travelers.

Charles H. Stearns served as New Mexico Prohibition director before opening the Country Club Court at 2411 West Central Avenue in 1937. Harvey Kruse took over in 1941. Later owners included Mr. and Mrs. W. D. Bolton and M. R. and Dorothea Smidt. It became the Prince Motel/ Relax Motel and is still in business as the 21 Motel.

This view of the Pueblo Bonito Court at 2424 West Central Avenue dates from 1943, when most tourist courts were being used as housing for defense workers. In 1961, owner Joseph Napoleone added a dome over the swimming pool, the first of its kind on Route 66. The court stood into the early 1970s, and a restaurant now occupies this site.

KATSON'S DRIVE-IN   ALBUQUERQUE, N. M.

Bob Katson, owner of the Court Café, opened his drive-in at 2425 West Central Avenue on May 18, 1940. It offered curb service by uniformed waitresses. Due to wartime shortages, it closed in September 1942 "until Hitler's funeral." It never reopened. The site became the Beacon Club after World War II.

Convenient to Downtown and
Historic Old Town Plaza

El Vado
Motel
2500 Central S.W. — On Highway 66
ALBUQUERQUE, NEW MEXICO

Private Swimming Pool For Guests

Dan Murphy, former manager of the Franciscan Hotel, built the El Vado Motel in 1936. Patrick O'Neill operated the motel from 1963 to 1986, and it closed on October 22, 2005. After a battle with a developer who wanted to tear down one of the best-preserved motels on Route 66, the City of Albuquerque took over the property in 2008.

A new bridge across the Rio Grande west of Old Town was completed in 1931 and became part of Route 66 in 1937. This four-lane bridge opened in October 1952. In 2002, the City of Albuquerque erected two Route 66 gateways west of the Rio Grande. A full arch spans West Central Avenue between Sixty-fourth and Sixty-fifth Streets.

Sandia Motel
On U. S. Highway 66 — 3416 West Central
ALBUQUERQUE, NEW MEXICO

The Sandia Motel at what is now 4618 West Central Avenue opened in 1947 and was offering kitchenettes for $15 per week in 1954. But it had fallen on hard times in the 1970s, advertising "XXX movies" and "mirrored luxury everywhere you look from your sumptuous water bed" in 1978. The Sandia Peak Inn stands on the site today.

Billed as "New, Modern and Distinctive" with Franciscan furniture, the Dutch Motel at 5401 West Central Avenue had 20 units. Owners included Mr. and Mrs. Otto Schmitt, Mr. and Mrs. W. L. Davidson, Mr. and Mrs. Irving Lewis, the Anthony Sullivan family, and H. L. Utz. It later became El Molina Motel but no longer stands.

The Hill Top Court opened in 1946 at 4010 (now 5410) West Central Avenue. Later the Hill Top Lodge, it was torn down in 2005. It was owned by Mr. and Mrs. C. T. Orton and later owned by Mr. and Mrs. J. Navra, advertising 25 rooms with "hot and ice cold water in abundance." The sign later advertised "refrigerated air."

The Cactus Lodge, later the Cactus Motel, at 5930 West Central Avenue consisted of 12 units offering "everything for your comfort." Mr. and Mrs. Bernard T. Feltman owned the motel in the 1950s, and the motel was later owned and operated by Mr. and Mrs. Don Lee. The Cactus Motel no longer stands.

The Sky Court was located at 4300 (now 5940) West Central Avenue. In July 1952, a new street numbering system divided the city into four quadrants, with Route 66 and the Santa Fe tracks as dividing lines. Businesses on this part of West Central Avenue received new addresses. The Sky Court no longer stands.

La Hacienda was known as the motel with the sunken garden at 6214 West Central Avenue. It originally had 18 units and expanded to 21 in 1955. While operated by Vincent and Gloria Brunacini, it advertised a location "on top of the West Mesa, where it is cool, comfortable and quiet." The sunken garden is gone, but the motel is still there.

James Hubbell was the grandson of John Lorenzo Hubbell, the famous American Indian trader whose home is now a historic site on Isleta Boulevard in Pajarito. James operated the Hubbell Motel at 6512 West Central Avenue from its construction in 1946 until he died in 1964. The motel no longer stands. (Courtesy of Nancy Tucker.)

In 1927, a Phillips petroleum official and driver found a name for the company's new fuel when they noticed they were doing 66 miles per hour on Route 66 near Tulsa. Beginning in 1959, stations such as the Acoma 66 Service at 6920 West Central Avenue incorporated elements of a design by Frank Lloyd Wright, including the distinctive canopy.

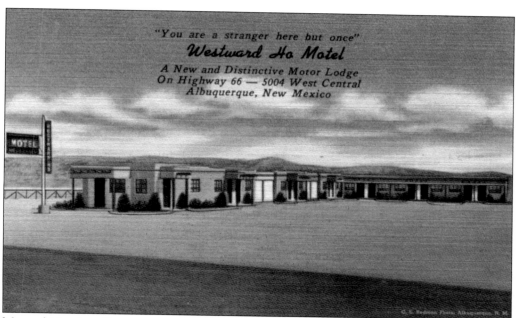

"You are a stranger here but once"

Westward Ho Motel

A New and Distinctive Motor Lodge
On Highway 66 — 5004 West Central
Albuquerque, New Mexico

Mr. and Mrs. Leo Zimmerman advertised "all drinking utensils individually sterilized" at the Westward Ho Motel, opened in 1948. It was later owned by Ed and Constance Keely. Constance made news when both of her daughters gave birth on her birthday, one in 1967 and the other in 1968. The Westward Ho, at 7500 West Central Avenue, is still open today.

The Grandview Motel at 9700 West Central Avenue was the first motel encountered by eastbound travelers inside the western city limits of Albuquerque. It was owned and operated by Russell H. Farber. The attractive motel is still in business today, with beautiful multi-colored neon on the rooflines.

This view looks east on Route 66 towards the Sandia Mountains from Nine Mile Hill. The crest of the hill is 9 miles from downtown Albuquerque. Travelers at night on eastbound Route 66 drove in darkness for many miles until they topped the hill to see the lights of Albuquerque spread out before them. A touch-up artist added the sign.

L. G. and Lena Hill's Hilltop Trading Post was 2 miles west of Nine Mile Hill. The Hills shut down and sued the New Mexico Highway Department after Interstate 40 construction left the trading post stranded on a frontage road miles from an exit. They originally were awarded damages but lost their case before the New Mexico Supreme Court in 1973.

Five

ALBUQUERQUE TO GALLUP

Originally G. D. "Doc" Hill's Midway Trading Post, the Tomahawk Trading Post was known for its Jimez Indian dances. Owner J. T. Turner stuck 10 phone poles made up to look like massive arrows around the property and constructed replica tepees next to the gas pumps. Turner operated several businesses, including the Buffalo Trading Post.

Morene and George Thomas Hill's Rio Puerco Trading Post was originally located on the south side of the highway just before Route 66 crossed the 1933 Rio Puerco bridge. After a fire in 1946, they built the store shown here on the north side. This building burned in the 1960s. The third building was torn down for Bowlin's Travel Plaza.

Route 66 cuts through the heart of the 42-square-mile Laguna Pueblo lands. The old highway twists around the beautiful rock formations that the builders of four-lane 66 and Interstate 40 simply blasted through. West of Mesita, Owl Rock still looms over the old road just east of another notorious stretch known as "Dead Man's Curve."

Laguna Pueblo was officially established in 1699, named after a nearby lake that no longer exists. The largest of the Keresan-speaking pueblos, it includes the villages of Laguna, Paguate, Encinal, Mesita, Seama, and Paraje. The San Jose de Laguna Church, completed in 1699, dominates the view of Kawaika, or Old Laguna.

About 15 miles south of Route 66 lies the "Sky City," Acoma Pueblo. It is the oldest continuously inhabited community in the United States, dating back to about 1075 AD. For thousands of years, it was accessible only by a staircase carved by hand into the nearly 400-foot-high sheer mesa. About 50 people live here today.

Howard Neil "Bud" Rice and his wife, Flossie, operated Budville, a trading company and station 22 miles east of Grants. Bud ran the only towing service on Route 66 between the Rio Puerco and Grants and was a justice of the peace criticized for his steep fines. Rice was shot and killed during a mysterious robbery on November 18, 1967, that some believe was a setup. Flossie ran Budville until 1979.

Wallace Gunn and Sidney Gottlieb ran the Cubero Trading Post. When Route 66 bypassed Cubero in 1937, they opened Villa de Cubero Trading Post and tourist camp on the new highway. Gunn's wife, Mary, ran the café across the street from 1941 to 1972. Local legend says Ernest Hemingway wrote parts of The Old Man and the Sea at the café.

Route 66 was still a dirt road when this view of the San Fidel Camp was made. San Fidel is virtually a ghost town today. But it is the home of Gallery 66, operated by Mary Trask and Mike Petzel. The art gallery occupies an adobe building constructed by Lebanese immigrant Abdoo H. Fidel in 1916 that was once the Acoma Curio Shop.

Route 66 passes through El Malpais, or "The Badlands" lava flows east of Grants. The sharp-edged lava flows cover over 300,000 acres. They slashed the tires of early motorists and presented a major obstacle to the early road builders. The old highway twists and turns to avoid the lava, while Interstate 40 simply cuts through.

Grants was originally a railroad base camp, established by brothers Angus, Lewis, and John Grant. It was known as Grant's Camp, then Grant's Station, and finally just Grants beginning in 1936. In 1950, rancher Paddy Martinez discovered uranium in the Haystack Mountains west of town, launching a 20-year-long mining boom.

The Grants Café opened in 1937. The 1958 sign shown here was abandoned miles away before it was returned and restored as part of the neon preservation project, a partnership of the New Mexico Route 66 Association, the New Mexico Historic Preservation Division, and the National Park Service Route 66 Corridor Preservation Program.

The 34-unit Franciscan Lodge at 1101 East Santa Fe Avenue in Grants opened in September 1950. Their motto was "The Best Costs No More." Owners Auro and Nellie Cattaneo went on to build the Desert Skies Motel in Gallup. In the 1970s, the Franciscan was owned by James and Pauline Pennington.

In 1956, the Lariat Lodge was advertised as "new and quiet." This card also boasted "unsurpassed comfort and complete accommodations for an enjoyable visit to the Uranium City." The 24-unit motel was a member of Congress Motels. The Lariat, located at 1000 East Santa Fe Avenue, became the Southwest Motel.

On U. S. Highway 66 — Grants, New Mexico

The 16-unit Grants Motor Lodge was opened in 1950 by E. King and later became the Grants Motel. Later owner Lawrence Essig was injured when a plane he was piloting crashed in 1954 and then died in a crash in January 1955. Erma Ableson took over in 1956. The site at 1009 East Santa Fe Avenue is now a storage business.

Red Prestridge, who also operated a logging company, owned the White Arrow Garage in Grants. This view shows the original building, which was remodeled and reequipped in February 1936. The garage also sold Ford automobiles. Prestridge sold the garage in 1960, and it remained in business into the 2000s. (Courtesy of Jim Coad.)

Milan is named for founder Salvador Milan. Salvador and his sister Mary were exiled from Mexico during the revolution in 1913. Mary married Walter Gunn, who ran the trading post at Villa de Cubero. Salvador built the Motel Milan with help from his brother-in-law Wallace Gunn in 1946. Note the inset showing the famous carrot fields.

This boy was photographed at Herman and Phyliss Atkinson's Lost Canyon Trading Post in 1948. The billboards, including one in the background promoting the "giant prehistoric reptile 48 ft. long," are for the Rattlesnake Trading Post, located a few miles to the west and operated by Herman's brother Jake.

The Lost Canyon Trading Post originally just included a couple of nonpoisonous snakes in "The Den of Death" and a three-legged bear named Bruno. Herman Atkinson began adding exotic reptiles, including a king cobra. The snakes proved so popular that Herman decided to concentrate on exotic reptiles starting in 1950. (Courtesy of Jim Coad.)

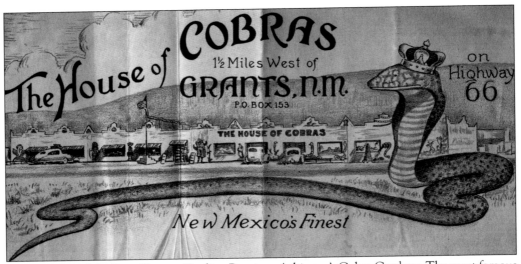

Herman turned the Lost Canyon Trading Post into Atkinson's Cobra Gardens. The most famous of all the Route 66 reptile attractions, it had the largest collection of cobras in the United States, including one that had killed a well-known herpetologist. The Atkinsons sold in 1954, and the snakes were moved to the Rattlesnake Trading Post.

Jake and Maxine Atkinson bought the Bluewater Trading Post from Victor Holmes in 1945. Holmes had tied burros to the pumps to lure tourists and staged cockfights. Jake opened the Rattlesnake Trading Post on the site, which also included a nightclub. He kept the cockfights going until he sold to Maxine's sister and her brother-in-law in 1951.

Tourists flocked to Rattlesnake Trading Post to see the 48-foot-long "giant prehistoric reptile" as advertised on billboards. In 1951, *Life* magazine used it as an example in an article entitled "How to trap a tourist." Jake Atkinson's monster was made out of cow vertebrae and plaster, with a horn stuck into a skull that was made out of a cow hip.

Johnnie and Helen Maich opened their café at Thoureau (pronounced "threw") in April 1927. They sold it to John and Anna Radosevich in 1936, just before Route 66 was rerouted to the other side of the tracks. The building was moved to the new alignment and was expanded in 1947. It is now Johnnie's Inn and the Red Mountain Market and Deli.

The Red Arrow Cottage Camp opened in 1922 on the rugged dirt road that would become Route 66. The cabins only included a bed and stove, with travelers sharing a washroom in the center of the complex. Note the swastika, an ancient religious symbol used by diverse cultures around the world, including the American Indians of the Southwest.

Top O' the World was a cluster of businesses on the Continental Divide that included Dee Westbrook's bar, known for its vicious cigarette-puffing monkey. Tourists were fleeced by shell games at the Top O' the World Hotel. By the 1960s, it was known for transients, bar brawls, and prostitution. The businesses here today are much quieter.

This was the view on the south side of Route 66 at Top O' the World. Bert Greer operated the Great Divide Trading Post. At 7,263 feet, the Continental Divide is the highest point on Route 66. Water that falls on the east side of the divide drains to the Atlantic Ocean, while rain on the west side drains toward the Pacific Ocean. (Courtesy of Jim Coad.)

The Navajo Lodge complex included a lodge, café and bar, store, and gas station. Merle and Daisy Muncy ran it from 1936 until World War II, when Al and Melvina Lavasek took over. They trained a pair of bears to guzzle Cokes bought by tourists. Roberta and Sherwood Stauder turned the lodge into a bed and breakfast. (Courtesy of Jim Coad.)

For roughly 40 miles between Grants and Gallup, the Route 66 traveler passes by amazing red sandstone rock formations. At center, the spires of Navajo Church Rock are visible. According to this postcard, the Navajo performed many of their ceremonies near Church Rock, now part of Red Rock State Park.

Six

GALLUP TO THE ARIZONA LINE

The Inter-Tribal Indian Ceremonial Association and the chamber of commerce erected this kachina statue promoting Gallup as the American Indian capital on Route 66 east of town in 1947. A smaller kachina at the west end of town said "Hurry Back." A similar figure now stands north of Interstate 40 at exit 22.

The Casa Linda Court, later the Casa Linda Motel, opened in 1937 at 2300 East Highway 66. Evelyn and John Simms ran what was known as "The Southwest's Model Auto Court" for over 20 years. It originally had 24 units and later expanded to 38. A restaurant was added in 1959. The Casa Linda no longer stands, and a McDonald's occupies the site today.

Earl Nelson was a Cherokee Indian from Oklahoma who opened Earl's Park 'n' Eat in 1947. Sharon Richards and her husband, Maurice, ran the restaurant at 1400 East 66 Avenue from 1974 to 1990, when they built Earl's Family Restaurant. The restaurant continues to please diners today.

The 40-room El Capitan Motel at 1300 East Highway 66 was opened by Dino Ganzerla in 1955. An advertisement for the motel said it was "Designed to Give You What You are Looking for in a Modern Motel." El Capitan was owned by Joe Di Pimazio in 1970 and is still in business today.

The Rivoli Café at 1200 East Highway 66 was known for excellent cuisine and good service. According to proprietor Ted Hodges, "our steaks and chops are exclusively broiled and our pizza pies, Italian and Mexican dishes are second to none. Your stay in Gallup will be enjoyable if you make the Rivoli café your headquarters."

John Milosovich of Gallup was the youngest mayor in the United States when he was elected in 1935 at age 21. His friend, lumberyard owner John Novak, offered to help with financing if Milosovich built a motel. The 20-unit Blue Spruce Lodge opened in 1949 and was such a success that Milosovich quickly paid his friend back. It is still in business.

The Arrowhead Lodge was completed in June 1949 at 1115 East Highway 66 and was owned by Mr. and Mrs. M. R. Francisco. The lodge was advertised as "offering unsurpassed comfort in large and roomy accommodations. Featuring Serta springs and mattresses, panel ray heat and carpeted floors." The Arrowhead still stands.

On July 4, 1952, the 35-room Lariat Lodge opened at 1105 East Highway 66. The back of the card reads "Howdy Pardner! Welcome to one of the Indian Capital's newest and finest lodges." The original sign with the cowboy and his lasso was replaced in the 1950s. But the second neon sign is still one of the coolest in Gallup.

The Avalon Café opened in 1945 at 1104 East Highway 66. Jack Soo Hoo took over in 1956 and introduced fine Chinese food to Gallup. The Uptown Plaza Shopping Center, opened in 1957, is in the background. This building no longer stands. The business became the Avalon Restaurant, now located at 1310 East Highway 66.

Formally opened on December 17, 1937, El Rancho Hotel was built for R. E. Griffith, supposedly the brother of movie magnate D. W. Griffith. It was the headquarters for 18 movies filmed between 1940 and 1964. Stars who stayed at the "World's Largest Ranch House" include John Wayne, Ronald Reagan, Katherine Hepburn, and Kirk Douglas.

Business dwindled after Interstate 40 opened on October 8, 1980, and El Rancho closed in 1987. The landmark was slated for demolition until Armand Ortega stepped in and restored El Rancho. The two-story lobby with its circular staircase and heavy beams is filled with Navajo rugs, mounted animal heads, and photographs of Hollywood stars.

This view looks east from Route 66 at Coal Avenue, the East "Y." Gallup was established in 1881 and named for railroad paymaster David Gallup. Workers would "go to Gallup" for their pay. Route 66 originally followed Railroad Avenue, turning south on First Street to Coal Avenue, meeting Railroad Avenue again at the West "Y."

Pete's Café and Club at the East "Y" formally opened on November 20, 1945. James Theopholis bought it in 1950 and opened Pete's Fine Foods here in 1959. Paris "Pete" Derizotis took over in 1960. The building later became the Talk of the Town Lodge and was occupied by a pawn shop as of 2010.

Several vintage tourist courts, including Redwood Lodge, El Coronado Motel, and the Zia Motel, are still clustered at the East "Y." The Zia was advertised as "a modern motel," with 26 units, including 13 with kitchen facilities and large airy rooms that were "homelike, comfortable and quiet." The motel still stands at 915 East Highway 66.

The All States Auto Camp opened in 1938 at 608 East Highway 66. The 19-unit court was originally owned by Dino Ganzerla, who went on to own El Capitan Motel. Some old structures that served as the original Overland Stagecoach stop stood on the grounds of the All States until 1947. The motel no longer stands.

Trading post owner Mike Kirk was greeted with skepticism when he proposed a gathering of the American Indian tribes to attract tourists. But the annual Inter-Tribal Indian Ceremonial has been a major attraction since 1922. American Indians come from all over North America for arts and crafts, sports, parades, and dances. In this photograph, the Santa Fe Railway's Indian Band is taking part in the big parade.

Peter Kitchen's Opera House hosted dances, concerts, boxing matches, and labor rallies, but no operas. It opened in 1895, and the upstairs hall closed in 1952. George Taira took over the restaurant on the first floor and named it the Eagle Café in 1922. It would be owned by people of Japanese descent into the 1990s and is still in business today.

H-1892 EL NAVAJO, SANTA FE HOTEL, GALLUP, NEW MEXICO. (AFTER PAINTING BY FRED GEARY)

The Fred Harvey Navajo Hotel opened on May 26, 1923. Harvey's chief architect, Mary Colter, created a spectacular blend of modern architecture and Native American culture. During the glory years, the famous Harvey Girls served 500 meals per train at least four times per day. El Navajo closed on May 25, 1957, and was demolished.

This view looks East on Coal Avenue (then carrying one-way Route 66 traffic) at Third Street (U.S. 666). At left is the City Electric Shoe Shop, which was operated by the Bonaguidi family and is still in business today. R. E. Griffith, who built El Rancho, operated the Chief Theatre. The Oldsmobile dealership at right became the Coal City Pub.

Jimmy Blatsios opened the White Café in December 1919 in the Heller Building at Railroad Avenue and First Street. He constructed this building with beautiful decorative brick, reopening the café in October 1929. The landmark building now houses an American Indian jewelry and artwork store. (Courtesy of Jim Coad.)

Years before Route 66 was laid out, the Manhattan Café was in business on Railroad Avenue. It moved to a new building at 304 West Coal Avenue after a 1927 fire. The Manhattan was known for its Indian Room and was operated for many years by Gus Anison. In 1943, it opened at 222 West Coal Avenue, a building occupied by a frame shop in 2010.

Dan Brunetto and Dominic Bertinetti's Ideal Auto Camp opened in May 1928. It became the Ideal Auto Court, ran by Bert Eddies. The Texaco station was later remodeled to incorporate elements of Dorwin Teague's classic design, and the motel units were changed to match. The site is now a Ford dealership used-vehicle lot.

The Paramount Café opened in 1950 at 904 West Highway 66 and was operated by the Pappas family. Milton and Mazie Mueller were running the Paramount when this view was taken. They advertised "Good Food is our Specialty" and promised the café was "large enough to serve you and small enough to want you." It was torn down in 2008.

Frank Leight's West Side Campground, the first tourist camp in Gallup, opened in April 1925. Frank named the station after Maggie and Jiggs and the cabins after other comic strip characters. The camp offered "everything a motorist needs except bedding and kitchen ware." It became the West Side Auto Court by 1935. (Courtesy of Jim Coad.)

Harry and Ivy Woodman invited travelers to "Stay Downtown" at the Cactus Motel. It originally had 14 units and was later expanded to 35. The classic sign featured a neon giant saguaro cactus, even though the nearest real giant saguaro would have been about 150 miles away. The motel at 809 West Coal Avenue no longer stands.

The Colonial Motel opened in 1956 and was advertised as "Gallup's newest and most modern." Mr. and Mrs. F. D. Bridges operated the 26-room motel when this view was made. They invited guests to "stop here for real comfort." The Colonial Motel is still in business today at 1007 West Coal Avenue.

Tony and Francis Leone opened the Log Cabin Lodge in July 1938. It originally consisted of six cabins. Two double cabins and an adobe-style wing were added during the 1940s and 1950s. After closing in the 1990s, it deteriorated into a haven for transients. Much of the complex burned in April 2004, and the rest was demolished.

Advertised as "Strictly Modern," 24-unit Pine Tree Lodge opened in 1953 at 1115 West Highway 66. Rooms rented for $7 per night. In 1958, AAA described it as a very pleasant motel, remarking that the "well furnished rooms are nicely kept." The Pine Tree Lodge was also a Best Western Motel. It no longer stands.

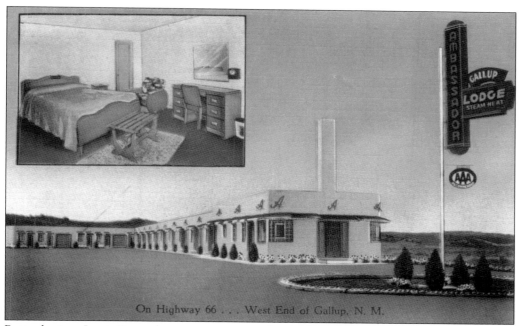

Retired miner Louis Bartot began constructing the Ambassador Lodge at 1601 West Highway 66 in 1946. Advertised as "One of Gallup's finest tourist courts," the Ambassador originally had 16 rooms and later expanded to 33. By 1959, it was known as the Ambassador Motel, and it is still in business today.

The ultramodern Desert Skies Motor Hotel at 1703 West Highway 66 opened in May 1959 and was operated by Auro and Nellie Cattaneo. The 34-unit motel boasted 21-inch televisions in every room along with hi-fi music. It is still in business today as the Desert Skies Motel, and the impressive sign still stands.

Earl Vance owned the Ranch Kitchen Restaurant in Farmington, New Mexico. The owner of the Thunderbird Lodge in Gallup asked Vance to open a restaurant adjoining the lodge. It opened in the summer of 1954 and became known as the home of the massive Navajo Taco. The restaurant moved further west in 1982, closed in 2005, and reopened in 2006.

The Thunderbird Lodge at 1811 West Highway 66 was named after the sacred North American Indian symbol for the bearer of happiness. Opened in 1955, the motel was owned by Don Wofford. It was owned later by the Cosper family, who founded Thunderbird Supply, and by Delbert Garrett. The Thunderbird no longer stands.

The Shalimar Hotel opened in April 1960 at 2015 West Highway 66, within walking distance of the airport. It was originally owned by Spencer Moss. The Shalimar had 84 rooms, later expanded to 124, and a golf driving range out back. It was later known as the Shalimar Inn, which closed in 2001 and was demolished in 2006.

Route 66 passes through Manuelito and then offers a view of the railroad. The arroyos of the Rio Puerco and Interstate 40 all crowd together in the narrow valley between the mesas on either side. The road rises and clings to the steep side of Devil's Cliff, with only a mesh fence protecting drivers from massive boulders.

Leroy Atkinson opened his Box Canyon Trading Post in 1943, luring tourists with a midget steer, shrunken heads, a zoo, and Native American craftsmen at work. Leroy sold after losing his gas pumps in a bitter battle with highway officials over right of way for the widening of Route 66 in 1953. Interstate 40 later wiped out what was left.

The mystical Harry "Indian" Miller opened the Cave of the Seven Devils in 1931 with a zoo and fake American Indian ruins. Miller once lived among the Philippine headhunters and had killed a man at his previous enterprise at Two Guns, Arizona. The Chief Yellowhorse Trading Post retains the feel of a classic roadside attraction on this site today.

The State Line Trading Post was the last stop in New Mexico, opened by Jake and Leroy Atkinson in 1940. For years, officials weren't sure if the post was in New Mexico or Arizona. Armand Ortega's first job was at the State Line. He went on to own an empire of trading posts across the Southwest and to restore El Rancho Hotel in Gallup.

www.arcadiapublishing.com

Discover books about the town where you grew up, the cities where your friends and families live, the town where your parents met, or even that retirement spot you've been dreaming about. Our Web site provides history lovers with exclusive deals, advanced notification about new titles, e-mail alerts of author events, and much more.

MADE IN THE USA

Arcadia Publishing, the leading local history publisher in the United States, is committed to making history accessible and meaningful through publishing books that celebrate and preserve the heritage of America's people and places. Consistent with our mission to preserve history on a local level, this book was printed in South Carolina on American-made paper and manufactured entirely in the United States.

This book carries the accredited Forest Stewardship Council (FSC) label and is printed on 100 percent FSC-certified paper. Products carrying the FSC label are independently certified to assure consumers that they come from forests that are managed to meet the social, economic, and ecological needs of present and future generations.

FSC
Mixed Sources
Product group from well-managed
forests and other controlled sources

Cert no. SW-COC-001530
www.fsc.org
© 1996 Forest Stewardship Council

Find Your Place in History.